AF102952

The Legend of Sleepy Hollow

A Play
in Two Acts

Based on
Washington Irving's
Classic Tale

CHRISTOFER COOK

Columbus, Ohio

This book is a work of fiction. The names, characters and events in this book are the products of the author's imagination or are used fictitiously. Any similarity to real persons living or dead is coincidental and not intended by the author.

The Legend of Sleepy Hollow: A Play in Two Acts

Published by Gatekeeper Press
3971 Hoover Rd. Suite 77
Columbus, OH 43123-2839
www.GatekeeperPress.com

Copyright © 2017 by Christofer Cook

All rights reserved. Neither this book, nor any parts within it may be sold or reproduced in any form or by any electronic or mechanical means, including information storage and retrieval systems without permission in writing from the author. The only exception is by a reviewer, who may quote short excerpts in a review.

ISBN: 9781619849099

Library of Congress Control Number: 2017957501

Printed in the United States of America

CAUTION

PROFESSIONALS AND AMATEURS ARE HEREBY warned that *The Legend of Sleepy Hollow*, A Play in Two Acts (Based on Washington Irving's Classic Tale) by Christofer Cook is subject to a royalty. It is fully protected under the copyright laws of the United States of America, and of all countries covered by the International Copyright Union (including the Dominion of Canada and the rest of the British Commonwealth), and of all countries covered by the Pan-American Copyright Convention and the Universal Copyright Convention, and of all countries with which the United States has reciprocal copyright relations. All rights, including (but not limited to) professional, amateur, motion picture, recitation, lecturing, public reading, radio broadcasting, television, video or sound taping, the world wide web, internet, social media, live-streaming, all other forms of mechanical or electronic, reproduction, such as information storage and retrieval systems and photocopying, and the rights of translation into foreign languages, are strictly reserved. Particular emphasis is laid upon the question of readings, permission and terms for which must be secured from the author. The aforementioned rights have been in effect since 2002, are in effect now, and are forever in effect for eternity, in perpetuity throughout the universe.

The stage performance rights for *The Legend of Sleepy Hollow*, A Play in Two Acts (Based on Washington Irving's Classic Tale) by Christofer Cook are controlled exclusively by the playwright. No professional nor non-professional performance of the play may be given without obtaining, in advance, permission by the playwright and paying the requisite royalty fee. All inquiries can be referred to;

Christofer Cook
101 Saluda Pointe Court #127
Lexington, SC 29072
HighVoltageSC@aol.com
(803) 429-8839

SPECIAL NOTE

ANYONE RECEIVING PERMISSION TO PRODUCE *The Legend of Sleepy Hollow*, A Play in Two Acts (Based on Washington Irving's Classic Tale) by Christofer Cook is required to give due authorship credit to the playwright as the sole and exclusive author of the play in all programs, posters, flyers, and any and all other promotional printing in connection with performances of the play. In all instances in which the title of the play appears for purposes of advertising, publicizing, or otherwise exploiting the play and/or a production thereof; the name of the author must appear on a separate line, in which no other name appears, immediately beneath the title and in size of type equal to 50% of the largest letter used for the title of the play. No person, firm nor entity may receive credit larger than that accorded the author.

The Legend of Sleepy Hollow made its world premiere in 2002, and subsequently, its most recent incarnation (at the time of this publishing) October 27th, 2017 at Village Square Theatre in Lexington, South Carolina. Directed by Debra E. Leopard, Produced by Jaime B. Pressor, Scenic Design by Matt Marks, Scenic Art by Carrie Marks, Costume Design by Nancy Huffines, the cast was as follows;

Ichabod Crane	Christofer Cook
Diedrich Knickerbocker	David Reed
Katrina Van Tassel	Kira Nessel
Abraham ("Brom Bones") Van Brunt	Sam Hetler
Baltus Van Tassel	Mark Dinovo
Mrs. Van Tassel	Andi Cooper
Hans Van Ripper	TJ Daley
Mrs. Van Ripper	Debra E. Leopard
Vanderghast/Andre/Starkenfaust	Jeffrey S. Sigley
Judith Gardenier	Stephanie Walker
Peter Vanderdonk	David LaTorre
Yost Van Houten	Joe Culley
Nicholaus Vedder	Jonathan Fletcher
Mrs. Vedder	Tabitha Davis
Parson Brouwer	Jerry Freeman
Snow Maiden	Blakesley Rhett
Derek Van Bummel	Paul Woodard
Jonathan Doolittle	Noah Marcum
Levi Van Helsing	Cameron Eubanks
Lars Van Gogh	Austin Burke
Doffue Martling	Daniel Woodard
Hilda Martling	Deedi Durst
Kristina Van Ripper	Mikaylin Price
Apparition #1	Virginia Walker
Apparition #2	Elise Heffner

Apparition #3 .... Brooke Buckner
Headless Horseman .... Cameron Swaim

Children,,,,,,Katie Riddle, Simone Y. Howard, Elizabeth German, Maddie Freeman, Lauren Weed

ACT I

ACT I

Breakdown of Scenes

Scene 1. "Dutch Settlers" 9
Scene 2. "Living Scarecrow" 13
Scene 3. "Architect by Design" 19
Scene 4. "Class Dismissed" 23
Scene 5. "No Room at the Inn" 25
Scene 6. "A Singing Master" 37
Scene 7. "Fireside Tales" 47
Scene 8. "Levitation" 55
Scene 9. "The Gift" 57
Scene 10. "An Exhibition of Bones" 59
Scene 11. "The Challenge" 65
Scene 12. "Swords are Crossed" 69

Scene 1.

"Dutch Settlers"

(AT RISE IT IS AUTUMN, 1795. A small valley near the banks of the Hudson River in the upstate of rural New York. The play opens as an appropriate moment in pre-show music gives way to the darkening of the house and an eerie supernatural light rising upon the stage. Soft, mysterious music, orchestral and ghostly in nature, fills the air as fog creeps in. Light reveals a tree in the background center. It is tall and gnarled with twisted branches that reach out towards the audience like the arms of an old witch. It is the tree upon which Major Andre, a British revolutionary war officer, was hanged for treason.

The entire set is a beautiful and haunting representation of a colonial Dutch village. Present are the front door stoops of the Van Tassel home at far stage left, the undertaker's parlor, next door closer to center, then the Vedder Inn at center stage, then stage right of center the Van Ripper's barn, and as room allows, the representation of the steps and double doors of the old Dutch church at far right. Everything appears old, primitive, decayed, homespun, and aged with tints of ghastly gray, mossy green, moldy sludge, and earthy browns.

Rusted farm implements stand near the barn, a wagon wheel as well, pine straw ground, with leafy clumps accent the stage, a few weathered signs adorn the requisite businesses such as 'The Vedder Inn', 'Vanderghast, Undertaker', and the most prominent sign of all, wooden, rotting and hanging by rusty chains, is 'Sleepy Hollow, 1795'. In small letters, one can include 'Population __' and include the number of the members of the cast. Most important of all in the style of Colonial Dutch, is the presence of several dormer windows (practical with shutters) on the sides of the little houses. Throughout appropriate moments in the play, warm, glowing light should emanate from the houses windows, smoke from chimneys if practical.

Gentle music eases in with warmer lighting to reveal Knickerbocker at an old writing desk in a non-specific corner of the stage picture. He strikes a match to light an oil lamp nearby. The ambient light-level intensifies as if conjured by *some magical power. Knickerbocker pulls out a quill and opens a journal. He lights his pipe and blows a smoke ring which rises and dissolves into the ether like an apparition. He begins writing his story as he addresses the audience. Music should continue to underscore his soliloquy and the action on the stage.*

Lighting rises upstage to again reveal the village as introduced in the prologue. Inhabitants of Sleepy Hollow gradually enter, one by one, some a few at a time. As they appear, their movements should be slow, fluid, and dreamlike as if they are ghosts of a time and place, long ago. As each inhabitant ends up at his/her respective home, he/she begins pantomiming a specific chore or pastime as is appropriate to each character; ie, Katrina can be picking apples from her family's grove, the Van Rippers can clean a horse saddle, Brom Bones can chop wood, Van Houten can study plans, etc. Eventually, the entire village is filled with silent inhabitants performing tasks in slow motion.)

KNICKERBOCKER

IN THE BOSOM, OF ONE of those spacious coves that indent the eastern shore of the Hudson River, there lies a small market port by the name of Tarry Town. Not far from this village, there is a little valley, known for the peculiar character of its inhabitants, who are descendants from the original Dutch settlers. It is one of the quietest places in the whole world. A small brook glides through it, with just murmur enough to lull one to repose, and the occasional whistle of a quail, or tapping of a woodpecker, is almost the only sound that ever breaks in upon the uniform tranquility. *(Enter boy as young Knickerbocker with a gun almost twice his size.)* I recollect that when a stripling, my first exploit in squirrel shooting was in a grove of tall walnut trees that shades one side of the valley. I had wandered into it at noontime, when all nature is peculiarly quiet, and was startled by the roar of my own gun!... *(There is a loud shot. At this, a few townspeople go to the boy to congratulate him on his kill. One woman takes him by the ear and leads him off. The villagers slowly and gradually exit.)* …as it broke the Sabbath stillness around and was prolonged and reverberated by the angry echoes. From the listless repose of the place, a drowsy, dreamy influence seems to hang over the land, and to pervade the very atmosphere

(Enter Sleepy Hollow boys). Its rustic lads, Brom Bones, Derrick Van Bummel, and Jonathan Doolittle are called the "Sleepy Hollow Boys" throughout all the neighboring country.

Scene 2.

"Living Scarecrow"
(Traveling music for Ichabod Crane.)

KNICKERBOCKER

NOW, IN THIS BY-PLACE of nature, there abode, in a remote period of American history, that is to say, some thirty years since, a worthy wight by the name of Ichabod Crane.
 (Ichabod enters with a long staff balanced over one shoulder and all his worldly possessions tied up in a cloth bag, fastened to the end of it. He also carries a small stack of books bound together by a leather strap.)
 He sojourned, or as his expressed it, "tarried" in Sleepy Hollow for the purpose of instructing the children of the vicinity. He was tall, but exceedingly lank, with narrow shoulders, long arms and legs and hands that dangled a mile out of his sleeves. Upon the stranger's arrival emerged from the wood a most enthusiastic or shall I say "appreciative" welcoming committee.
 (Knickerbocker exits. As Ichabod sits upon a tree stump to wipe his weary brow, the "Sleepy Hollow Boys" approach.)

BROM BONES
Do my eyes deceive me?! It appears to be a living
scarecrow eloped from a cornfield!

DERRICK
I think it's a corpse from the churchyard in search of a good meal.

BROM BONES
What do *you* say, Jonathan?

JONATHAN
It's a ghost! Can't you see his skin, white as a sheet?

ICHABOD
My dear fellow –

BROM BONES
It speaks!

ICHABOD
Well of course I speak. I am of the fortunate, yet sadly few, who can boast of being fully literate. I speak English, Latin, German, French, Italian, as well as your native Dutch.

DERRICK
And from whence do you hail, stranger?

ICHABOD
I am a native of Connecticut.

JONATHAN
A Yankee!

ICHABOD
Careful, careful. It is a state which supplies the country with pioneers for the mind as well as the forest. It sends forth yearly its legions of frontier woodsmen and country schoolmasters.

DERRICK
The scarecrow is a state publicist to boot.

ICHABOD
Ichabod Crane, Pedagogue.

BROM BONES
Crane? Of course! A CRANE!!! Look, lads,
we've got a giant fowl on our stump!

(The boys do their best bird imitations.)

ICHABOD
Now, see here.

DERRICK
A crane, a crane!

JONATHAN
A crane, a crane!

BROM BONES
Come now, Mynheer. Do you not admit your name is rather fitting?

ICHABOD
I concur. The cognomen of my surname is not inapplicable to my idiosyncratic corpus.

BROM BONES
I can't tell whether he agreed with me or not.

DERRICK
Indeed, the strange bird speaks a language not our own. I see his beak moving but I can't understand a word he's chirping.

BROM BONES
A rare breed. Derrick, take notes.

(Van Bummel pulls out a sheet of parchment and a quill and begins writing down all that Brom Bones dictates.)

BROM BONES

We may have an endangered species on our hands. A talking crane, and foreign-tongued at that!

DERRICK
All right then, dear Doctor Bones, please dictate.

BROM BONES

Upon closer examination, the subject's frame is most loosely held together by dangling wings, stalky legs, and feet that may well serve as shovels. His head is small, and flat at top, with huge ears, large, green, glassy eyes, and a long snipe nose.

JONATHAN
Is that a nose or a beak?

BROM BONES
Not sure.

DERRICK
Perhaps it's a weathercock, perched upon his spindle
neck to tell which way the wind blows.

BROM BONES
To see him striding along the profile of a hill on a windy day…

JONATHAN
…with his clothes bagging and fluttering about him…

DERRICK
…one might mistake him for the genius of famine…

BROM BONES
…descending upon the earth!

(The boys burst into hysterical laughter, and begin flapping their own 'wings', cawing and flying in a circle about Ichabod.)

Scene 3.

"Architect by Design"

(YOST VAN HOUTEN ENTERS. HE is an eccentric architect whose apparel tells the story of a bachelor more obsessed with his profession than his appearance. He sees what is happening and saves the helpless Ichabod Crane.)

YOST
Alright, you vagabonds! Enough! Enough! Let the poor man alone. Away with you!

(The boys run off mocking Crane. They each have a stick have a stick to his own shoulder, and a handkerchief to his brow. Their movements are exaggerated and grotesque. They explode into laughter as they exit. Van Houten approaches Crane.)

ICHABOD
Thank you, kind sir.

YOST
Pay them no mind. There's more mischief than ill will in their composition.

ICHABOD
Pardon, Mynheer. But, I'm looking for the schoolhouse. You see, I'm the new schoolmaster and I understand the facility is somewhere nearby. Do you know it?

YOST
Know it, my good man? I designed it.
(He extends his hand. Ichabod shakes it.)
Yost Van Houten. Architect.

ICHABOD
Ichabod Crane. Pedagogue.

YOST
A pleasure, a pleasure. Now, the schoolhouse is a low building of one large room, rudely constructed of logs; the windows partly glazed, and partly patched with leaves of old copy books.

ICHABOD
Oh, my. It sounds rather Spartan. You see, I have many books that I'd hoped to store there. Is the schoolhouse quite secure?

YOST
It is most ingeniously secured at vacant hours, by a withe twisted in the handle of the door, and stakes set against the window shutters; so that though a thief might get in with perfect ease, he will find some embarrassment in getting out. An idea I borrowed from the mystery of an eelpot.

ICHABOD
Well, that should be sufficient. And how do I find it?

YOST
Follow this road apiece until you come to a clearing. The schoolhouse stands in a rather lonely but pleasant situation, just at the foot of a woody hill. You'll see a brook running close by, and a formidable birch tree growing at one end of it.

ICHABOD
Thank you, Mynheer.

YOST
My pleasure!!! Oh, and if you should happen to need services of an architectural nature, here's my calling card. I can provide speculations, renderings, and plans at no extra charge.

ICHABOD
Thank you, Mynheer. I'll keep that in mind.

(A final handshake and Van Houten exits. Crane loops around during Knickerbocker's speech and "finds" the schoolhouse.)

KNICKERBOCKER
Ichabod found the birch tree and the schoolhouse. As time passed and days turned into weeks, the Yankee schoolmaster settled into a comfortable routine. At the end of a crisp Autumn school day, Ichabod Crane was known to remind his students that the birch tree outside was not only a thing of beauty but served for utilitarian purposes as well.

(Knickerbocker Exits.)

Scene 4.

"Class Dismissed"

(KNICKERBOCKER EXITS. HOUSELIGHTS RISE A bit to illuminate the 'schoolhouse'. Crane addresses the members of the audience as they become his students. He threateningly wields his birch switch for emphasis.)

ICHABOD

Pupils! As you've just been witness to the administering of justice at the expense of Master Van Rotten, the birch tree outside is not only a thing of beauty, but also serves for utilitarian purposes as well. Now, now,… Don't think that I cannot hear the low murmur of your voices, conning over your lessons like the hum of a bee's hive. I can. And I shall be apt to interrupt your rumbling with the voice of your master. A sound you may interpret as authoritative, commanding, menacing. But let me give assurance, nothing will speak so plainly as the voice of this little twig of birch as I urge *you*, tardy loiterer, along the flowery path of knowledge. You'll learn that I am conscientious and ever bear in mind the golden maxim 'spare the rod and you spoil the child'. You, my little scholars, will certainly not be spoiled. Don't think, however, that I enjoy the doling out of punishment upon your backsides. I am not one of those cruel potentates who joy in the smart of their subjects. On the contrary, you'll find I administer justice with discrimination rather than severity. The innocent foil to a guilty party's shenanigans will be passed by with indulgence, yet the claims of justice will be satisfied by inflicting a double portion on some little, tough, wrong-headed, broad-skirted Dutch urchin. *(At this he places the Dunce cap on some unsuspecting member of the audience.)* Oh, you can sulk and swell and grow dogged and sullen beneath the birch. But all this is simply doing my duty by your parents. And I will never inflict a chastisement without following it by the assurance that you will remember it and thank me for it, the longest day you have to live. *(He pulls out a pocket watch and checks the minutes of the hour so as not to release the students a second early.)* Class… is… now… dismissed!

(Crane vigorously rings his hand-bell to signal the closure of another school day. Knickerbocker enters.)

Scene 5.

"No Room at the Inn"

(ICHABOD GATHERS HIS THINGS, GRABS his stick with sack on the end, puts his hat on and heads to the front stoop of the Vedder Inn.)

KNICKERBOCKER

Up until now, Ichabod Crane had taken up residence at the home of the reticent Nicholaus Vedder, a patriarch of the village and landlord of "The Vedder Inn". It was a fine country boardinghouse whose weekly rate became more of a burden than the pedagogue could carry.

(Enter Crane followed by Mrs. Vedder, then Nicholaus. The three come from the direction of The Vedder Inn.)

MRS. VEDDER
We're so sorry you have to leave us, Mynheer Crane.

ICHABOD
The revenue arising from my school is small and scarcely sufficient to furnish me with room and board. Therefore, I'm afraid I can no longer afford your fine accommodations.

MRS. VEDDER
This comes as most unwelcome news. You were such a tidy boarder. Perhaps if we were to lower your weekly contributions. Couldn't we do that, Dear?

(Nicholaus Vedder says nothing, but continues his unsettling stare of disapproval at Crane. Ichabod senses the tension and jumps in.)

ICHABOD

No, Mevrouw Vedder. I'm afraid I cannot ask you to do that. You have already given me a most reasonable rate and I will take advantage of your good graces no longer. I will have to refuse your kind offer.

MRS. VEDDER

But, where will you go, Mynheer Crane? We simply can't throw you out onto a dirt road like a common vagrant. Can we, Dear?

(Again, Nicholaus says nothing, but imagines the possibilities as he puts his clay pipe between his teeth.)

ICHABOD
I am resourceful, Mevrouw.

MRS. VEDDER
(Considering his statement)
Yes, well, nonetheless…
Perhaps we can assist you in finding affordable lodging.

(In Crane's traveling music, the three make their way to the funeral parlor of Mort Vanderghast, undertaker of Sleepy Hollow.)

KNICKERBOCKER

The Vedders, being compassionate to Ichabod's plight, promptly dispatched him to the one place they knew he could find a nice, satin pillow, stretch out his legs, and not be disturbed by his fellow boarders. They introduced him to Mort Vanderghast, undertaker of Sleepy Hollow.

(Music continues throughout the brief action in which no dialogue is spoken. When they arrive, Mrs. Vedder pulls a string at the back of Vanderghast's business which rings a bell. Vanderghast steps out, having been interrupted in the middle of his work. He wears a long, brown apron absolutely caked with

the blood and fluids of his "clients". There can be no doubt whatever, about the nature of his profession. Vanderghast is seen greeting the visitors warmly. They don't take his hand, rather they all nod politely. The Vedders gesture to Crane as if making the necessary introductions. They wave 'goodbye' and leave the scene, heading back to the Vedder Inn. Vanderghast removes his apron and hangs it on a rusty nail. The two men are in the middle of conversation when the music and narration ends.)

MORT
I think I understand, Mynheer Crane.

ICHABOD
The arrangement would be temporary, Mynheer Vanderghast. As my appointment as School Master has just commenced, I will find independent lodging upon my first weekly compensation.

MORT
You can stay as long as you like. Just remember, this is no inn. No bed linen here, only shrouds.

ICHABOD
Shrouds?

MORT
No fresh-cut tulips to smell, only a pocket full of posies. You'll grow accustomed to the stench.

ICHABOD
Stench?

MORT
And I've no dining quarters here. You'll have your morning repast in the casket parlor.

ICHABOD
C-C-Casket parlor?

MORT
It's all I've got. You can use a display coffin for your breakfast table. Just close the box firmly, sit down and eat. When you're done, wipe the lid down with a damp cloth. Then be on your way, as we hold visitations in the afternoon.

ICHABOD
I'm not sure…

MORT
And one other thing… If you arrive long after dark, the oil lamps may have been snuffed out. Be careful where you bed down. Wouldn't want you to wind up on the wrong table, now would we?

ICHABOD
Wr-Wr-Wr-Wrong table?

(The bell rings, signifying another client. Ichabod is startled.)

MORT
Nothing to worry about, Master Crane. I'll give you a tour of the place when I return.

ICHABOD
I think I'll just be…

MORT
I go and it is done: the bell invites me.

Fear it not, Mynheer; for it is a knell
That summons us to Heaven or to Hell.

(The bell rings more loudly this time.)

MORT

I only hope its someone trying to get in, and not trying to get out. If you follow my meaning. Please, excuse me, Master Crane.

(He exits into his parlor. Crane, clearly shaken by the prospect of rooming in Vanderghast's mortuary, begins to have second thoughts. Throughout mysterious music, Crane peers in through Vanderghast's windows, snoops around the front, picking up a gravedigger's shovel. He then puts it aside in fear. He peeks inside an unfinished, empty coffin which Vanderghast had been building. He finds a simple wooden cross for a pauper's grave. He lifts it and holds it in front of him as if practicing to ward off evil spirits. He then bends over to place it back into the coffin. Vanderghast suddenly bursts through his door, slamming into Crane's bum and sends the schoolmaster face-first into the coffin. This jostling causes the lid to slam shut. Crane screams from within as Vanderghast bursts into laughter. He lifts open the lid to help the poor man out.)

MORT

Oh, my dear Master Crane! Get out of there! It's a bit early for that, if you follow my meaning.

(Vanderghast has now helped Crane completely out of the coffin.)

ICHABOD
Thank you, Mynheer Vanderghast.

(Vanderghast helps to brush sawdust off Crane's shoulders.)

Need you attend to your business?

MORT

False alarm. Turns out old man Bummel wasn't dead at all. Only intoxicated. Now, how about that tour?

ICHABOD

I sincerely thank you, Mynheer Vanderghast. Your hospitality is most humbling. However, I have reconsidered and I cannot accept. You see, the Reverend Cotton Mather, of whom I am a loyal disciple, is a most notable and honorable authority in the dynamics of the hereafter. I'm afraid he would not approve. A living soul abed in a mortuary would create a most potent alchemy for the devil's playground. And witches and devils have no place in a house of the dead.

MORT

You've nothing to worry about here, Mynheer. My business is one of sanctity.

ICHABOD

All the same, if you could be so kind as to suggest an alternative dwelling?

MORT

Very well. I could refer you to the Van Rippers. They are simple ranchers who may have a spare loft. I'll take you to them. It's too bad really. I think you might enjoy learning about the processes of death. *(Suddenly becoming morose as eerie music eases in. Ichabod actually hears the music and looks about briefly as if to discover its origin.)* I've watched men die, you know. It's a beautiful thing in its own way. The bed of death, with all its stifled griefs – the last testimonies of expiring love! *(He grabs Crane's hand, as though he himself is in the throws of expiration.)* The feeble, fluttering, thrilling – oh! How thrilling! – pressure of the hand! The faint, faltering accents, struggling in breath to give one more assurance of affection! The last fond look of the glazing eye, turned upon us even from the threshold of existence!... *(Pause, Vanderghast appears to come back into this 'world'. Underscoring music suddenly ends.)* You sure you won't reconsider?

ICHABOD
I don't think so.

(Crane's traveling music.)

KNICKERBOCKER
And so it was, Vanderghast aimed to help out Ichabod's maintenance. The schoolmaster was, according to country custom in these parts, boarded and lodged at the home of one of the farmers whose child he instructed. Vanderghast, being compassionate to his plight, promptly dispatched him to the barn of Heer Hans and Mrs. Van Ripper.

(Hans, the Mrs., and Kristina appear from the barn. Vanderghast makes silent movement as if to introduce Crane to the Van Rippers, he then exits.)

MRS. VAN RIPPER
We are happy to take you in, Mynheer Crane.

ICHABOD
Juffrouw Kristina is an apt pupil and I'm sure that my presence in your home shall make an honorable impression upon the child.

HANS
Yes, about your accommodations.
You won't exactly be living in the house, per se.

ICHABOD
Oh?

MRS. VAN RIPPER
Do you like farm animals, Mynheer Crane?

ICHABOD
Well, I prefer my cattle medium rare, on a steaming plate, with a sprig of parsley for garnish, if that's what you mean?

HANS
No, that's not what we mean.

MRS. VAN RIPPER
Your room is,…

HANS
Let's call it a "rustic" quarters.

MRS. VAN RIPPER
It's a damp stable.

KRISTINA
But we have a dry bed of hay.

HANS
It's well-ventilated.

MRS. VAN RIPPER
Cracks in the walls and loft.

KRISTINA
But we'll give you blankets.

HANS
Now, Loves, you make it out to be a pauper-shack. It isn't as though we've never kept boarders.

MRS. VAN RIPPER

That's true. We have. Four horses, three geese, a few hogs, goats, chickens…

KRISTINA

…and mice!

HANS

So, you'll have a little company.

ICHABOD

I can't thank you enough, Mynheer Van Ripper, Mevrouw Van Ripper, Juffrouw Kristina.

MRS. VAN RIPPER

Well! Would you like to unpack your effects, Mynheer?

ICHABOD

Fine.

MRS. VAN RIPPER

Are you hungry?

ICHABOD

No, no thank you. I'm not hungry. A small thimble of water will be sufficient… well, all right, a crust of bread. But I don't want to put you out. Perhaps, though, a chop or two of mutton, and maybe Brussel sprouts on the side with a dollop of fresh cream or butter on top. A potato couldn't hurt, and then perhaps a flagon of Jenever to wash it all down.

HANS

I'm just glad he isn't hungry.

ICHABOD
It has been said of me that although I am lank, I am a healthy feeder and possess the dilating powers of an anaconda.

HANS
Welcome home, Ichabod Crane.

(Crane peeks his head in the barn. A loud mooing of a cow is then heard which startles Crane. He tosses his belongings in.)

ICHABOD
It will do nicely. How shall I ever repay you?

MRS. VAN RIPPER
Well, since you asked. That your teaching services might not be too onerous on the purses of your patrons, who are apt to consider the costs of schooling a grievous burden, and you a mere drone…

HANS
There are various ways by which you may
render yourself both useful and agreeable.

(Van Ripper tosses a harness in Crane's arms.)

Oil the tack!

(Doffue grabs the harness and hands Crane a pitchfork.)

DOFFUE
Bail the hay!

(Nicholas grabs the pitchfork and hands Crane a hammer.)

HILDA
Mend the fences!

(Hans grabs the hammer and hands Crane a hoe.)

HANS
Muck the stalls!

(Brouwer grabs the hoe and hands Crane a crop.)

BROUWER
Drive the cows from pasture!

(Mrs. Van Ripper grabs the crop and hands Crane a bucket.)

MRS. VAN RIPPER
Fill the troughs!

(Yost grabs the bucket and hands Crane a hatchet.)

YOST
Cut wood for the winter fire…

(Mrs. Van Tassel grabs the hatchet and hands Crane a basket.)

MRS. VAN TASSEL
…and harvest the crops!

(Mrs. Van Ripper grabs the basket, and hands Crane a book. Hans places Kristina on Crane's lap, Mrs. Van Tassel puts a small wooden cradle at Crane's foot. Mrs. Vedder hands Crane a bowl of porridge with a spoon.)

MRS. VAN RIPPER

You'll sit with a book, feeding a child on one knee while rocking another to sleep with your foot. We're off to market!

(She exits with the other ladies. Knickerbocker enters wearing a choir robe. During Knickerbocker's following monologue, Parson Brouwer and several singing members of the cast appear as townspeople in matching robes and take their position around Crane for singing.)

Scene 6.

"A Singing Master"

KNICKERBOCKER

IN ADDITION TO HIS OTHER vocations, he was the singing master of the neighborhood. When school hours were over, he would indulge in this, his seemingly more lucrative enterprise. Ichabod Crane would pick up many bright shillings by instructing the young folks in psalmody. On Sundays he would take his station in front of the church gallery, with a band of chosen singers; where, in his own mind, he completely carried away the palm from the parson.

(Knickerbocker joins the rest of the choir as Parson Brouwer raises a baton. There is an excited hustle and bustle and general hubbub amongst the choir. Brouwer has to quiet them down.)

PARSON
Brothers,… Now, Sisters… Attention, please! Thank you. Sing nice and full this Sabbath and delight the congregation in the fruits of our labor. Now, let's all come together and lift our voices to the Lord. Ready? Voices up!

(He taps his baton and leads the group in a musical psalm. It is Kremser, from Nederlandtsch Gedenckclank, 1626. ["We gather together to ask the Lord's blessing"] acapella, well-sung, simple and with nice harmony. It should be hauntingly beautiful. Ichabod's voice appropriately rises above the others. It is, however, too nasal and loud to be ignored. The song comes to a close.)

PARSON
That will do for now. If you'll bow your heads, we'll ask the good Lord to bless us. *(All bow their heads, reverently.)* Dear Heavenly Father, we ask your blessing

upon our humble voices this morning. Let us make a joyful noise unto you. Be us ever mindful of Isaiah, chapter 35, 6th verse, when you said "The tongue of the dumb shall sing!" Amen. The parishioners should be arriving soon. I will meet you all in the sanctuary. Remember, voices up! Voices up!

(Parson Brouwer dismisses everyone and heads to the church doors. Crane crosses downstage to center, where he'd previously left a small stack of books. He clumsily begins to gather them as the choir group gradually make their way into the church. Katrina stays behind to join Ichabod. Baltus Van Tassel pulls Brom Bones aside.)

BALTUS
Abraham, my boy.

BROM BONES
Yes, Mynheer Van Tassel?

BALTUS
Still sparking for my daughter, Katrina?

BROM BONES
Respectfully, yes, Mynheer. Though it appears I have competition.

BALTUS
Never you mind. I've a few ideas.

(As they head to the church, Baltus takes Brom Bones by the arm and whispers in his ear.)

KATRINA
Have you read *all* these books, Mynheer Crane?

ICHABOD

Yes, Juffrouw. I have read several volumes quite through. *(He shows her his favorite book.)* and I am a perfect master of Cotton Mather's "History of Witchcraft, a New England Almanac", in which, by the way, I most firmly and potently believe.

(Katrina takes the book from him and thumbs through its pages.)

KATRINA

Witchcraft? Do you practice as well?

ICHABOD

Good Heavens, No! It's merely a fascination. Around here a person can get put to death for mere suspicion of witchery.

KATRINA

I wouldn't worry. We haven't pressed anyone to death in almost a hundred years.

ICHABOD

True enough.

(Katrina finds a chapter title in the book that interests her. She reads aloud.)

KATRINA

"Spells of Love and Enchantment"? Is this how you win the hearts of women?

(He gently takes the book from Katrina's hands and closes the cover. He packs it away.)

ICHABOD

I profess not to know how the hearts of women are wooed and won. To me, they have always been matters of riddle and admiration.

KATRINA
And what am I? A woman to be riddled? Or admired?

ICHABOD
You, Katrina, are one to be cherished.

KATRINA
That's very sweet, Mynheer Crane, but…

ICHABOD
Oh, Ichabod. Please.

KATRINA
Alright, Ichabod. But what assurance have I that you don't shower such niceties to *all* your female students of psalmody?

ICHABOD
None, I suppose. But I say nothing without sincerity.
I'll never lie to you, Juffrouw Van Tassel.

KATRINA
Katrina, please. Do I have your word?

ICHABOD
You have my word as a gentleman. And that's a sure beginning.

KATRINA
Indeed. Honesty is the way to a woman's heart.

ICHABOD
Good to know. Women's hearts are oft impenetrable. They seem to have but one vulnerable point of access.

KATRINA
Not all. Some have countless avenues,
and maybe captured in a thousand different ways.

ICHABOD
And you? Does your heart possess so many portals of entry?

KATRINA
Well, the only way to discover the entrance to a castle is to turn the key in every lock. And if that fails, storm the breach like Prince Hal. For a man must battle for his fortress at every door and window. He who does less lacks heart, nobility, courage. He is no man at tall. But he who fights for what he wants is a knight in my book. He who reigns supreme over the heart of a woman is indeed a hero… Are you a hero, Ichabod?

ICHABOD
That depends. Are you a battlement to be conquered?

KATRINA
You answered a question with a question. They say people who do that are manipulative. What do you think about that?

ICHABOD
What do *you* think I think about that?

(They both laugh.)

KATRINA
That's very good. You're clever.

ICHABOD
And you're perceptive.

(The church bell rings. Katrina starts to go in. Judith Gardinier, a purveyor of meats and vegetables, enters with a small push cart of produce. She observes Ichabod and Katrina discreetly.)

KATRINA
May your cleverness win you the heart of a fair maiden.

ICHABOD
And may your perception find you a hero.

KATRINA
You'll be the first to know.

(Katrina is at the church doors.)

ICHABOD
Do I have your word?

KATRINA
You have my attention, Ichabod. And that's a sure beginning.

(Katrina exits. Judith steps into the scene.)

JUDITH
A fine catch for some fortunate gentleman.

ICHABOD
I beg your pardon?

JUDITH
The young lady with whom you were speaking. Was it not Juliet's nurse who reasoned, "He that can lay hold of her, shall have the chinks"?

ICHABOD
Indeed it was… The lass comes from a prominent family to be sure.

JUDITH
Indeed. She stands to inherit all that her father doth possess. I should know. I service the Van Tassel cupboard.

(Extends her hand to Crane. He takes it.)

Judith Gardinier. Purveyor of fine meats and vegetable fare.

ICHABOD
Honored, Juffrouw Gardinier. Ichabod Crane, Pedagogue.

JUDITH
You are, no doubt, familiar with the Van Tassel estate?

ICHABOD
Yes, but my heart yearns after the damsel who is to inherit those domains.

JUDITH
Katrina Van Tassel.

ICHABOD
Even she!

JUDITH
So tell me truthfully. Is it your heart which yearns, or your purse?

ICHABOD
Why whatever are you suggesting?

JUDITH

If you hadn't known she was the daughter and only child of the substantial, wealthy Dutch farmer, Heer Baltus Van Tassel, would you still be so taken by her?

ICHABOD

Juffrouw Gardinier, certain it is, every relationship has its,…shall we say, fringe benefits?

(Judith gestures outward as if seeing all that she describes. Ichabod's eyes follow.)

JUDITH

There it is, all for the taking! The plantation of Heer Van Tassel! Look upon that sumptuous promise of luxurious winter fare! Picture to yourself every roasting pig running about with a pudding in his belly and an apple in his mouth; the pigeons snugly put to bed in a comfortable pie, and tucked in with a coverlet of crust. The geese are swimming in their own gravy; and the ducks pairing cozily in dishes like snug married couples.

ICHABOD

Snug married couples?! Is that how they are?

JUDITH

Roll your great, green eyes over the fat meadowlands, the rich fields of wheat, of rye, of buckwheat, and Indian corn, and orchards…

(She sticks a ripe, red apple in Ichabod's mouth. He pulls it out and takes a bite.)

…burthened with ruddy fruit, which surround the warm tenement of Baltus Van Tassel!

ICHABOD

The Van Tassel Orchards!

JUDITH

Expand your imagination with the idea how they might be readily turned into cash, and the money invested in immense tracts of wild land, and shingle palaces in the wilderness.

ICHABOD

Nay, my busy fancy is already realizing my hopes!

JUDITH

Imagine, you and the blooming Katrina with a whole family of children, mounted on the top of a wagon loaded with household trumpery, with pots and kettles dangling beneath; and you yourself bestriding a pacing mare, with a colt at her heels, setting out for…

ICHABOD

Kentucky, Tennessee,…

JUDITH

Or the Lord knows where!

(Ichabod suddenly snaps out of his fantasies.)

ICHABOD

Just what is *your* interest in my prosperity?

JUDITH

I trust you'd remember the little people who helped you along?

ICHABOD

I do believe the Latin phrase is "Quid Pro Quo".

JUDITH
Commerce, Mynheer Crane. Simple Commerce.

(She grips the handles of her push cart and rolls it off to Exit.)

ICHABOD
But I haven't paid you for the apple, Judith Gardinier!

(Judith turns back to him with a knowing smile.)

JUDITH
You will.

(She exits.)

ICHABOD
Till we meet again, Juffrouw!

Scene 7.

"Fireside Tales"

(A GRADUAL MUSIC BRIDGE AND lighting change between scenes signifies it is later in the evening. Ichabod goes directly to the pre-set area of Mrs. Van Ripper's parlor. Mrs. Van Ripper, Mrs. Van Tassel, Mrs. Vedder, Katrina Van Tassel, and Judith Gardinier are cozily spinning yarn for quilts and roasting apples on a fire. Ichabod Crane sits amidst the ladies with a cup of hot tea in his hands. He holds court.)

MRS. VEDDER

We are so fortunate to be graced with the presence of such an astute and learned man.

MRS. VAN TASSEL

You are always welcome to indulge in this, another source of your fearful pleasures.

JUDITH

Passing long, cold evenings by the fire with us.

MRS. VAN RIPPER

Mynheer Crane, you've made quite an impression
amongst our circle of ladies.

ICHABOD

Mevrouw Van Ripper, I cannot tell you what an auspicious honor it is to be in your home, among you fine ladies as you sit spinning in the parlor, a row of apples roasting and spluttering along the hearth.

MRS. VAN RIPPER

The pleasure is ours, Mynheer Crane.

KATRINA

I told you he was as entertaining a raconteur, as he is a singer.

MRS. VAN TASSEL

We so enjoy your fascinating talks on Galileo,
Astronomy, and the laws of gravity!

ICHABOD

Indeed, I have many interesting theories and speculations on comets, shooting stars, and the vast universe which enraptures ordinary man with it mystery.

KATRINA

Why just the other day, Heer Crane was telling me that the earth doesn't at all sit still as so many would have us believe, but it actually moves!

MRS. VAN TASSEL

The earth moves?

MRS. VEDDER

Is it possible?

MRS. VAN RIPPER

Do tell us, Mynheer Crane!

ICHABOD

Well, to put it plain,… the earth upon which we all reside, is simply one monolithic ball in the hands of God. But gravity, a physiological precept conjured by the creator himself, holds mankind firmly to the globe's crust like a gigantic magnet. After long hours of careful meditation on the subject, I have concluded that the world absolutely turns round and round and that we are half the time, topsy-turvy!

ALL
Simply amazing! That's incredible! Alarming! I don't believe it!

ICHABOD
Oh, yes! It's all true, Miladies. But such unexplained phenomenon perhaps is not the most appropriate subject matter for you more refined womenfolk.

(Ichabod stands, as if to pour another cup of hot tea. The ladies quickly jerk him back down to a seated position again.)

ALL
What?! Pshaw! The devil you say! Oh, no?!

MRS. VAN TASSEL
These environs are as appropriate a place as any for tales of the unnatural.

(Foreboding music creeps in, lights begin to dim, and the ladies all slowly turn their heads to face front. Their demeanor has obviously changed as they've lost their smiles and their expressions betray that of stiffened corpses. Ichabod notices the lighting and sound change, as well as the hypnotic state of the ladies. He is spooked.)

JUDITH
We can regale you with many strange tales of ghosts and goblins…

KATRINA
…haunted fields…

MRS. VAN RIPPER
…haunted brooks…

MRS. VEDDER
…haunted bridges…

MRS. VAN TASSEL
…haunted houses…

MRS. VEDDER
And of course the galloping Hessian of the Hollow, or as he is most often referred, "the headless horseman"!

ICHABOD
(Visibly un-nerved.)
Hea-hea-hea-head-less horseman?

MRS. VAN RIPPER
Now, Mynheer Crane. Surely you know of the Hessian trooper.

ICHABOD
No, but I have a feeling you're all about to enlighten me.

MRS. VEDDER
It is said that one soldier decapitated in the war and vengeful because of the act, rises from his crypt, horse and all, and seeks out the soul responsible for his death.

MRS. VAN TASSEL
He has been heard several times of late, patrolling the country.

MRS. VAN RIPPER
He tethers his horse nightly among the graves in the churchyard.

MRS. VEDDER
And wields a sickle or saber to lop off the head of
anyone he suspects is the culprit.

KATRINA

Parson Brouwer himself had an encounter.

JUDITH

Yes, he met the horseman returning from his foray into Sleepy Hollow and was obliged to get up behind him. On they galloped over bush and brake, over hill and swamp until they reached the old bridge when the horseman suddenly halted. threw old Brouwer into the brook, and hurled his own severed head in the direction of the Parson. The Hessian turned 'round and vanished. Parson Brouwer, by the grace of God, lived to tell the tale.

ICHABOD

How did he survive?

MRS. VAN TASSEL

The bridge itself is a nexus between this existence and the underworld.

KATRINA

It is said the horseman cannot cross the structure lest his demon spirit be hurled back into Hell.

JUDITH

…and his presence in this world, vaporize.

MRS. VAN RIPPER

And so it is, anyone pursued by the goblin rider can survive so long as he makes it to the other end before the headless creature can attack.

KATRINA

The innocent, would-be victim escapes, riding off into the night, and the horseman always turns back toward the cemetery.

MRS. VEDDER

Old Brouwer has oft described the demon spirit. He is dark. Dressed in black. The fleshy folds of skin where once his head joined his body have begun to rot. But the wound itself still appears fresh. The muscle fiber from the throat is exposed. Gurgling sounds can be heard through his windpipe as blood flows freely from the open hole at the base of his neck.

(Suddenly music goes out and lighting restores. The ladies all snap back into their friendly characters.)

MRS. VAN RIPPER
More cranberry sauce, Mynheer Crane?

ICHABOD
No, Mevrouw Van Ripper, I believe I've had all I can stomach.
At it *is* getting rather late.

(Ladies all rise simultaneously.)

ALL LADIES
Leaving so soon?!

(Startled, Ichabod nearly jumps out of his skin.)

ICHABOD
Yes, I must be going now!

MRS. VAN TASSEL
Oh, and we so wanted to hear more about your methods in pedagogy. There's so much still that we have yet to know about you.

JUDITH
The most important thing about Mynheer Crane
is that he is worthy husband material.

(The ladies love the comment and all react accordingly. Ichabod feigns embarrassment.)

ICHABOD
Now, Judith!

JUDITH
I'm acquainted with him well enough.
I'll tell you all that I know over more coffee.

MRS. VAN TASSEL
Shall we to the kitchen, then?

JUDITH
Come, Katrina. I think you'll find what I have to say equally of interest.

KATRINA
All right.

MRS. VAN TASSEL
Very well. Goodnight, Mynheer Crane.

KATRINA
Goodnight, Ichabod.

(Mrs. Van Tassel, Katrina, and Judith make their way to the kitchen. Mrs. Van Ripper and Mrs. Vedder lag behind to clear some dishes.)

ICHABOD
By the way, at just what hour is sunrise?

MRS. VAN RIPPER
Mynheer Crane, our barn is only down the old dirt road apiece. You'll be safe in your bunk and fast asleep before you know it.

ICHABOD
Yes, I'm sure you're right. Good evening, miladies.

MRS. VEDDER
Pleasant dreams.

(Ominous music creeps in. The two ladies exit. Ichabod Crane dons his hat and scarf and ventures out into the night. Foreboding sounds of the dark woods surround him. He startles and quakes with each new and terrifying sound.)

ICHABOD
Whatever comfort the Van Ripper's crackling wood fire gives, where no spectre dares show his face,… It is dearly purchased by the terrors of my subsequent walks homeward, however brief to their barn. What fearful shapes and shadows beset my path amidst the dim and ghastly glare of a chill-filled night! How I am thrown into complete dismay at the idea that every rushing blast or howling among the trees may be this galloping Hessian on one of his midnight scourings! I'll to my sleeping quarters as quickly as,…

(A flash of lightning followed by a crackle of thunder.)

Scene 8.

"Levitation"

(SUDDENLY, JUST AS ICHABOD BEGINS *his hike towards the Van Ripper's barn, he catches sight of a light on in the schoolhouse. Music becomes even more ominous and suspenseful.*)

ICHABOD

Oh dear! What's this? A light on in the schoolhouse?! I left no such lantern nor candle aflame this afternoon. This requires investigation by some brave and courageous person. And as such souls are in short supply here, I suppose *I'll* have to venture within.

(*Ichabod arrives at the schoolhouse. He opens the door, and immediately reaches for the crucifix hung by the doorframe. He holds it before him as he gingerly steps in to see what is causing the ghastly glow within. He is shocked by what he sees. Schoolhouse objects and furniture virtually appear to be in a slow state of levitation as they lift off the floor, desks, tables, and stools, and ascend as if by some invisible magical force. Picture frames slide upwards on walls, and make their way to the ceiling. Rising music accompanies the ascension.*)

Angels and ministers of grace defend us! What manner of black magic can render such objects unto this state of ascension? What creeping creatures have crept into my schoolhouse at night, in spite of Heer Van Houten's formidable fastenings? It is certain! All the witches in the country must hold their clandestine gatherings here. Oh horror of horrors!

(*The objects should now be at their highest possible point in the schoolhouse. Suddenly, from behind the schoolhouse unit, Brom Bones, Derrick Van Bummel, and Jonathan Doolittle appear. They are all holding on to the ends of ropes and it is clear that they are the ones who created the illusion designed to scare Ichabod out of his wits. They explode into laughter. Ichabod, nonplussed, sees the rope and puts it all together. The boys lower the objects.*)

BOYS
Booooowwwhhaaaahaaaaa!

ICHABOD
Ruffians!

(Startled, Ichabod screams and falls backward. Bones and his Sleepy Hollow boys begin making ghostly moans and caterwauls. They get up into Ichabod's face and then run off into the woods laughing hysterically all the way. Ichabod stands up and brushes himself off.)

ICHABOD
Morning cannot come quickly enough!

(He takes off in the direction of the barn. Knickerbocker enters.)

KNICKERBOCKER
Brom Bones drew upon the funds of rustic waggery in his disposition and played off boorish practical jokes upon his rival. Ichabod had become the object of whimsical persecution to Bones and his gang of rough riders. And in this way matters went on for sometime.

Scene 9.

"The Gift"

(HAPPY MORNING MUSIC WITH FRESH lighting change. Ichabod enters briskly hand-in-hand with Katrina. They spin about like a whirling dervish.)

ICHABOD
…but I suppose my favorite epitaph of all is that of William Shakespeare himself;

"Good friend, for Jesus' sake forbear
To dig the dust enclosed here.
Blessed be the man that spares these stones,
And cursed be he that moves my bones."

KATRINA
Why that's really, very,… *macabre*, Ichabod.

ICHABOD
I thought you'd like it. I have something for you.

(He hands her the almanac on the history of witchcraft.)

KATRINA
This is your copy of Cotton Mather's "History of Witchcraft, A New England Almanac".

ICHABOD
It's yours now. Keep it as long as I have your heart.

KATRINA
Thank you, Ichabod. I shall.
(In music of love, they run off together.)

Scene 10.

"An Exhibition of Bones"

KNICKERBOCKER

THE NEXT DAY, BROM BONES offered a show of physical prowess for all to see. It was clear that his secretive discussion with Baltus Van Tassel on Sunday morning and Ichabod's apparent courtship of Katrina led to the exhibition designed to steal the young girl's heart.

(Brom Bones enters with Jonathan Doolittle on his back. Derrick Van Bummel is not far behind. Bone's minions help to announce the exhibition with horns, banners, and other appropriate fanfare. Curious townspeople begin to appear. Ichabod Crane, however, is conspicuously absent from these next two scenes.)

BROM BONES

Good people of Sleepy Hollow, Tarrytown, and all parts from Greensburgh to the Tappan Zee! Let the exhibition begin! For behold! I have arrived! *(At this point the crowd has assembled around him.)* Before this day is done, I'll prove myself the only worthy suitor for the heart of one Katrina Van Tassel! For I, Abraham Van Brunt, am hero of the country road. My feats of strength and hardihood are known throughout this hollow, Tarrytown, and beyond! Let the exhibition begin!

MRS. VAN RIPPER

Why should *you* win the young Van Tassel's affection?

BROM BONES

Because I'm handsome.

MRS. VAN TASSEL
Can you carry firewood?

BROM BONES
For that, I'm broad-shouldered.

KATRINA
Can you write with both hands?

BROM BONES
Yes, I'm double-jointed.

(Laughter from the crowd.)

MRS. VEDDER
Are you strong?

BROM BONES
My frame is that of Hercules!

YOST
Have you a brain?

BROM BONES
I am famed for great knowledge in horsemanship.

HANS
But can you ride?

BROM BONES
I'm as dexterous on horseback as a Tartar.

BALTUS
Do you have a loyal heart?

BROM BONES
Indeed. There's only *one*, for whom *my* heart skips a beat.

MORT
And does your heart "skip-a-beat" in the figurative sense? Or the literal?... If you follow my meaning.

BROM BONES
I wouldn't be so hopeful, Mynheer Vanderghast. You'll be long gone before I'm a client of yours. I'm as healthy as a bear. But you toy with me. You all ask me questions for which you know the answers. I know what you think of me. You know what I think of myself. I want to know what Katrina thinks of me.

KATRINA
I think no more of you than I think of Ichabod.

BROM BONES
You'll agree I possess a bluff but not altogether unpleasant countenance?

KATRINA
Perhaps. But a man is only as fair as is proved by his actions.

BROM BONES
I'm very active! *(Laughter from the crowd)* I'll attend any scene of feud or merriment for miles around. I am foremost at all races and cockfights; I am always ready for either a fight or a frolic. When any madcap prank or rustic brawl occurs in the vicinity, you can warrant Brom Bones is at the bottom of it! In short, I'm arrogant, but fun!... Enough talk! Let the challenge begin! Will it be tomahawk throwing? Arm wrestling? Wood chopping? I am in form and spirit a supple jack – I am pliable, yet firm. Yielding, but tough. Though

I bend, I never break. At the slightest pressure, I roll, I jab, I swing, I sway, I make minced meat of my prey. Once victorious, I am erect and carry my head as high as ever! Now, be there any man alive who can best me? Shall it be the schoolmaster who'll accept my challenge? Let Ichabod Crane come forth and I will break open his pate like a gourd, I'll whip his innards into a Christmas pudding, I'll sling him about like an infant's plaything!

KATRINA

Why Heer Crane, Brom Bones? He's not so much as spoken a harsh word against you.

BROM BONES

He is my rival for your affections, is he not? I've seen the way he eyes your tender, yet desire-provoking… ankles. *(The crowd reacts with embarrassment as this is scandalous to mention in public.)* I've spied how he vies for your affections, and I've marked his poetic, yet pathetic attempts at courtship. Will you deny it?

KATRINA

No, I cannot deny it.

BROM BONES

Come then,…
(He throws one of his gloves to the ground.)

The gauntlet is tossed!

KATRINA

I'll answer on behalf of Heer Crane. He respectfully declines. He is too conscious of the superior might of his adversary to enter the lists against you. You have the obvious advantage, as your might displays. He therefore could not win such a match. Ichabod's prowess lies not in his physical strength, but in his mind, heart, and soul.

BROM BONES
Will he concede defeat, then?

KATRINA
No, he will not fight you, nor will he concede defeat. He shall win my love upon his own terms, not yours. And if I will accept his declarations, he will prove the better suitor. For we will soon see who can best speak the language of love. *(She picks up the glove and forces it to Bones' chest. He takes it.)* That is my challenge for you. Now, if you will all excuse me, I have a voice lesson.

(Katrina exits.)

BROM BONES
You see this, Derrick? Jonathan? Just as I suspected. No one man enough even to arm wrestle.

(The crowd, still as statues, simply stares silently at Van Brunt. He becomes angry.)

Well, what are you all staring at? You may as well go about your business! Is it not enough a man must be humbled by the girl he loves, but he must be publicly humiliated as well? Go on! There's no show here!

(The crowd dissembles and gradually the townsfolk make their way back to their homes, trades, etc. Brom Bones is left with Derrick Van Bummel and Jonathan Doolittle.)

Scene 11.

"A Challenge"

(JUST AS PETER VANDERDONK IS preparing to leave the scene, Van Brunt sees him. He speaks to Van Bummel.)

BROM BONES
Isn't that Van Tassel's gentleman?

DERRICK
'Gentleman'? More like Van Tassel's scrub-wench.

BROM BONES
What gripe have you with the man?

DERRICK
I don't recall.

JONATHAN
Don't you remember, Derrick? He beat you soundly in a game of cards?

DERRICK
It meant nothing to me.

JONATHAN
Yeah, but you cried. He made him cry. Don't you remember when you cried?

DERRICK
(Trying to ignore Jonathan's comment, Van Bummel speaks to Van Brunt.)
He's anyone's hired man. For a price.

BROM BONES
Then, let's put him to work.

(Van Bummel stops him.)

DERRICK
You! Vanderdonk!

(Peter Vanderdonk stops, turns around to face Brom Bones.)

PETER
I am Peter Vanderdonk.

BROM BONES
Will you deliver a message to the schoolmaster?

PETER
A message, Van Brunt? I trust it is worth a schilling.

(Brom Bones snaps his fingers at Jonathan, who pays Vanderdonk from his own pocket.)

BROM BONES
At least. Tell Ichabod Crane that if he wants the exclusive attentions of Katrina Van Tassel, he will have to best me first.

PETER
Vrouw Van Tassel has already indicated that he is a gentleman and will not fight you.

BROM BONES
Alright, fair enough. This Crane fancies himself a cavalier? Let us then compete using the weapons of true gentlemen… swords. Let's call it, "Best in

the Art of Swordplay". "Last Man Standing". Van Bummel will be my sparring partner and second. I suggest Crane take up lessons immediately. Let the duel commence at three of the clock this afternoon. Here.

PETER
Swords, Van Brunt?

DERRICK
That's what he said. Maybe you don't know what a sword is.

PETER
On the contrary. I was born with one in my right hand. And I shall be glad to deliver this message to Heer Crane. For I will offer *my* services as *his* partner in sparring and *his* second at the duel. Now, while your company is most engaging, I must leave you if Heer Crane is to prepare for your whipping at three of the clock.

(Vanderdonk turns to leave.)

DERRICK
You're an errand boy!

(The comment stops Vanderdonk in his tracks. He turns to Van Bummel.)

PETER
Yes, but I'm an errand boy with a rapier. Any time you want a message from me, I'll be sure to "deliver". Gentlemen.

(Vanderdonk exits. Van Bummel makes a move as if to lunge for Vanderdonk. Van Brunt stops him.)

BROM BONES

Pay him no mind. This is between Crane and myself. Let Vanderdonk school him in the art all he desires. He has only till the strike of three. I shall double the schoolmaster up and lay him on a shelf of his own schoolhouse.

(In music, the three exit. Enter Knickerbocker.)

KNICKERBOCKER

Such was the formidable rival with whom Ichabod Crane had to contend. And considering all things, stouter men than him would have shrunk from the competition. However, from the moment Ichabod made his interests known, a deadly feud gradually arose between him and the burly warrior of Sleepy Hollow.

Scene 12.

"Swords are Crossed"

(EXCITING BATTLE MUSIC. BROM BONES and Derrick Van Bummel, his practice partner, enter with fencing gear in the "courtyard" center stage. Ichabod Crane and Peter Vanderdonk , his practice partner, enter with cruder gear from the opposite side. The practice sparring ensues on both sides and Bones exhibits the swordsman skills of a master, while Crane barely knows which end of his weapon is to be held. While the four men are warming up in two separate locations, a few townspeople gradually enter, a few at a time. When the stage is ultimately full with the entire company of villagers, Brom Bones and Crane bump into each other's backs in the center. Crane makes an attempt to run away from Bones, cowardly. Bones pursues him. Crane dives into a crowd, the crowd then, toss Crane back into the melee with Bones. Crane does so with such speed that he ends up having leaped onto Bones' front like a frightened Koala bear. Bones shrugs him off, Crane falls to the ground at one point, supine. Derrick and Jonathan go to him, one crosses Crane's arms while the other places an Easter Lily in his hands. Vanderghast meanwhile stretches a tape measure from the top of Crane's head to his heels as thought to get an accurate measurement for his coffin. The crowd pulls the three away from Crane. More swordplay ensues, Crowd gets more loud and intense, music intensifies as well. Cheers and jeers from the villagers. The two fight until the scene climaxes in Bones getting the upper hand as Crane is disarmed, supine again, and exhausted. Bones positions a foot amidst Crane's chest in the traditional pose befitting a hunter with his kill. The crowd gives a final cheer, music reaches its crescendo, crowd freezes in a sudden tableau, lights out. Milder music begins and plays throughout intermission.)

END OF ACT ONE

ACT II

ACT II
Breakdown of Scenes

Scene 1. "The Van Tassels at Home" 73
Scene 2. "An Invitation" 81
Scene 3. "Gunpowder" 87
Scene 4. "He Designed it!" 91
Scene 5. "An Autumn Feast" 95
Scene 6. "War Stories" 101
Scene 7. "The Very Witching Time of Night" 105
Scene 8. "Three Apparitions" 107
Scene 9. "The Stalking Dead" 111
Scene 10. "The Headless Horseman" 115
Epilogue 117

Scene 1.

"The Van Tassels at Home"

(BALTUS AND MRS. VAN TASSEL are busy with preparations for their annual quilting frolic. Baltus cleans a basket of red apples. Mrs. Van Tassel is churning butter. They are in the midst of argument.)

MRS. VAN TASSEL
It's disgraceful!

BALTUS
Brom Bones won the duel fair and square.

MRS. VAN TASSEL
Be that as it may, it turned into a public spectacle much to the shame of Master Crane.

BALTUS
Crane accepted the duel!

MRS. VAN TASSEL
Abraham didn't need to embarrass the poor man.

BALTUS
My Love, a little embarrassment is the least of hazards endemic in a duel of swords. He could very well have killed the schoolmaster, after all.

MRS. VAN TASSEL
That's very nice, isn't it? We've come to battle of physical superiority over wits.

BALTUS
He accepted the duel!

MRS. VAN TASSEL
And you encouraged Abraham Van Brunt to compete for Katrina's interest!

BALTUS
I encouraged an exhibition of strength.

MRS. VAN TASSEL
You admit it!

BALTUS
I said nothing to him about a duel.

MRS. VAN TASSEL
You didn't have to. Young men are quick to interpret
an elder's words for their own purposes.

BALTUS
Abraham's a good lad. He only means to impress Katrina.

MRS. VAN TASSEL
At the risk of possible injury to our Hollow's schoolmaster.

BALTUS
It's over now.

MRS. VAN TASSEL
You'd do well to let Katrina's affections run their course, wherever they may.

BALTUS

It is true. I seldom send either my eyes or my thoughts beyond the boundaries of my daughter and farm.

MRS. VAN TASSEL

Yes, but within those boundaries everything is snug, happy, and well-conditioned We are prosperous enough and will remain so without worrying over who our daughter will one day choose to marry.

BALTUS

I am satisfied with my wealth, but not proud of it. There is a difference. While I do pique myself upon a hearty abundance, I make no gaudy show in the style that I live.

MRS. VAN TASSEL

I'm not denying that. I am simply saying the schoolmaster is more suitable for Katrina than the blacksmith.

BALTUS

Listen, I'm an easy indulgent soul. I love Katrina better even than my pipe. And like a reasonable man and an excellent father, I let her have her way in everything. But like most fathers, I am suspicious of the motives of every *stranger* who comes to court my daughter.

MRS. VAN TASSEL

Heer Crane is no stranger to Katrina.

BALTUS

Still. It's my duty to protect my daughter.

MRS. VAN TASSEL

Doesn't the farm keep you occupied? I have enough to do to attend to my housekeeping and manage my poultry. Therefore, I've learned that ducks and geese are foolish things and must be looked after, but girls can take care of themselves.

BALTUS
Can They?

MRS. VAN TASSEL
They can without the meddlesome interference of parents.

BALTUS
What's this Crane after, anyway?

MRS. VAN TASSEL
He has a soft and foolish heart toward the girl. Why should we wonder that so tempting a morsel finds favor in his eyes?

BALTUS
Tempting a morsel? She's our daughter, not a strudel!

MRS. VAN TASSEL
Of course, Dear. And Ichabod Crane is a red-blooded man no less subject to the allures of youthful beauty than is the blacksmith Abraham Van Brunt.

BALTUS
He makes his advances to her in a quiet and gently insinuating manner. His visits to our farm are more and more frequent.

MRS. VAN TASSEL
Voice lessons! He is, after all, her singing master.

BALTUS
It's a perfect ruse… Entering such a prosperous family would be quite a promotion for a schoolteacher, would it not?

MRS. VAN TASSEL

Baltus Van Tassel, you should be ashamed to even suggest that Master Crane has ulterior motives!

BALTUS

It happens, Dear. A stranger moves into the village. Professes his love for a well-to-do young vrouw. She gives her heart away. They marry. And before you know it, the fellow has moved in, inherited her father's wealth, and taken off for Amsterdam! I just don't want to be taken. More importantly, I don't want Katrina to be taken.

(Katrina enters and overhears the next question.)

MRS. VAN TASSEL
Give him a chance.

BALTUS
How old is this man, anyway?

KATRINA
Old enough to recognize suspecting parents a mile off.

MRS. VAN TASSEL
Your father has concerns over Master Crane's courtings of you.

KATRINA

You needn't worry, Vedder. Ichabod Crane is a man of vastly superior taste and accomplishments. Inferior in learning only to the Parson. Moeder, I want to invite Heer Crane to our festivity this evening. He deserves to join our frolic as much as Brom.

BALTUS
Invite him to the…!

MRS. VAN TASSEL

Let Katrina invite him to the merrymaking. It won't hurt to have Master Crane at our feast. Then you yourself can examine the gentleman more closely. You may find more in him than you realize.

(Baltus considers as he chews his pipe.)

BALTUS

He'll eat everything in sight, you know.

MRS. VAN TASSEL

There's plenty enough food for everyone.

BALTUS

Does he have to sing? Tell me he won't sing.

KATRINA

He won't sing. He may dance, but he won't sing.

BALTUS

Well, all right. Ichabod Crane is welcome to our autumn feast.

(Katrina wraps her arms around him and kisses his cheek. Mrs. Van Tassel lovingly rubs his back.)

KATRINA

Thank you, Vedder!

(She exits.)

MRS. VAN TASSEL

Thank you, Baltus. You're a good man.

BALTUS
Yes, I am.

(They exit hand-in-hand into the house. As they are exiting, Baltus adds…)

He's going to eat everything.

Scene 2.

"An Invitation"

(Ichabod is back in the school room. He addresses the audience.)

ICHABOD

Now, pupils! You see in my hand a familiar object, no doubt. Whether you believe it to be the scepter of despotic power or a birch of justice, I'll hang it here aside the 'throne' as a constant terror to evil-doers. *(He hangs the switch on a hook on the lectern, then picks up a wooden case about the size of a bread box.)* Now, here I have your various and sundry contraband articles and prohibited weapons confiscated from the bony little fingers of you idle urchins. Such as half-munched apples, popguns, sling-shots, whirligigs, fly cages, and whole legions of rampant, little paper gamecocks. As for the most recent transgression for which you were all complicit,… and don't pretend you can't recall. When last you were dismissed, books were flung aside without being put away on the shelves, ink-stands were overturned, benches thrown down, and you burst out of the schoolhouse like a legion of young imps, yelping and racketing about the green in joy at your emancipation. I assure you, today I'll not suffer the bustle and hubbub in this schoolroom. You will, like good scholars, pore over your lessons without stopping at trifles; those who are nimble will skip over half with impunity, and those who are tardy will have a smart application on the rear to quicken their speed or help them over a tall word. That being said, you will procure your chalk slates, and open your English literature books to Chaucer's *The Canterbury Tales*.

(Peter Vanderdonk comes running into the classroom, out of breath.)

PETER
Greetings, Mynheer Crane.

ICHABOD

Why Peter Vanderdonk! You are full of importance and hurry. What mission is so urgent that you would grace me with your presence this afternoon?

PETER

You're giving lessons, so I shan't be long. I am to deliver this.

(He hands Crane a folded parchment sealed with the wax imprint of the Van Tassel family crest.)

ICHABOD

Whatever could this be?

(Ichabod opens the letter and reads, silently.)

PETER

It's an invitation for you to attend a merry-making to be held this evening at the home of Heer Baltus and the family Van Tassel. I am sent at the bequest of the master of the house and Mevrouw Van Tassel.

ICHABOD

And the occasion?

PETER

A quilting frolic.

ICHABOD

This evening?! This is rather late notice.

PETER

Indeed, I suspect the invitation list was finalized just this morning. Even now all is bustle and hubhub at the estate for the preparations. It is to be a masked gathering.

ICHABOD
A masked gathering. Oh my!

PETER
The festivities are to commence at eight of the clock.

ICHABOD
Am I to assume that Brom Bones is also invited?

PETER
He is. Heer Van Tassel encourages the two of you to make merry in a neutral setting. In addition, he was heard to say that tapping a cask of Jenever may do us all some good.

ICHABOD
"Jenever" know!

(They both have a laugh.)

PETER
Very good, Mynheer.

ICHABOD
And am I to escort the young Van Tassel this evening?

PETER
The vrouw will be in attendance, Mynheer.

ICHABOD
Think you she intends to clutch mine arm?

PETER
She will be in attendance, Mynheer.

ICHABOD
But did she ask for me, in particular?

PETER
The invitation was sent from the Van Tassel household. Katrina Van Tassel certainly resides there. You may conclude it is from the young Katrina herself.

ICHABOD
Ah! Thank you, Peter! But,… She made no specific mention of Brom Bones, nor my name to you?

PETER
While she did not send for you personally, you were not excluded. Though she has not refused the advances of Van Brunt, neither has she accepted his attempts. Now, the vrouw did not specifically mention your name. But that is not to say your name did not cross the lips of the young lady. For I happen to know that her current book of natural wonders is turned to the chapter, "Orinthology"…

ICHABOD
Correct –

PETER
And any decent essay on birds must include the "crane", that wading fowl off our own New England coasts. And we all know that Katrina reads aloud. We can therefore assume Katrina has uttered the word "Crane" at least once this afternoon.

ICHABOD
Oh, this Katrina, she is clever! Why this is the very craft of young courtship. And it is a game derived to maintain the interests of her suitor. There is now no question but that the vrouw intends to make her declarations of love for me a public show. This is the very purpose of the "merry-making", or "quilting

frolic". The Van Tassel's fortunes are at hand! The savory-baked meats shall coldly furnish forth the marriage tables. A thousand thanks to you, Peter Vanderdonk!

(Crane pays him several bright schillings.)

PETER
And just as many to you, Mynheer Crane!

(Vanderdonk exits. Crane rings the handbell.)

ICHABOD
Class Dismissed!!!

(Ichabod Exits.)

Scene 3.

"The Van Ripper's Horse"

(Knickerbocker enters.)

KNICKERBOCKER

It was a fine autumnal day, the sky was clear and serene, and nature wore that rich and golden livery which we always associate with abundance. The forests had put on their sober brown and yellow, with tender trees tinted into brilliant dyes of orange, purple, and scarlet. Now, in order that gallant Ichabod might make his appearance before his mistress in the true style of a cavalier, he sought to borrow a horse from the rancher with whom he was domiciliated; the choleric old Dutchman, Hans Van Ripper. The pedagogue arrived at the Van Ripper paddock and issued forth like a knight errant in quest of adventures.

(The Van Rippers have entered in front of their barn. Hans, Mrs. Van Ripper, and Kristina are organizing horse tack. Knickerbocker exits as Ichabod enters.)

ICHABOD

Afternoon, good Landlords!

MRS. VAN RIPPER

You're home early, Mynheer Crane.

ICHABOD

I dismissed my students promptly, as I have to prepare for tonight's festivities at the Van Tassels.

HANS

Careful, Crane! You come out here to the barn, we'll put you to work.

MRS. VAN RIPPER
Ignore him. Everyone's entitled to one afternoon off.

ICHABOD
I'm here to request the use of your finest horse.

HANS
My finest horse?

ICHABOD
As I have been invited by Katrina Van Tassel to tonight's merrymaking, I had hoped that I might make my appearance before my mistress in the true style of a cavalier.

HANS
Very well, Crane. I'll loan you the finest horse that 'ere trod the hollow; "Gunpowder".

ICHABOD
Oh my! With a name like Gunpowder, he's sure to be full of fire and mettle!

KRISTINA
Don't get too excited.

HANS
Why he's a fine steed.

MRS. VAN RIPPER
He's a broken-down plow horse.

HANS
Plow, yes, plow! He's a beast of labor, full of viciousness!

MRS. VAN RIPPER
He's outlived everything else.

HANS
Yes, but he's lean and mean!

MRS. VAN RIPPER
He's gaunt and shagged

HANS
His head is unusually shaped…

MRS. VAN RIPPER
Like a hammer.

HANS
Now he's just a wee bit unkempt.

MRS. VAN RIPPER
His mane is rusty, is tail is tangled and knotted with burrs.

HANS
Yes, but he'll fix you with an eye of spirited fire!

KRISTINA
He lost the other eye long ago.

MRS. VAN RIPPER
It hangs a bit out of its socket. Lost its pupil and glares at you all spectral like. A thick, milky film oozes from the…

HANS
Alright, alright! Let's not oversell, Dear.

ICHABOD
Mynheer Van Ripper, might I borrow Gunpowder just for the night?

HANS
He's all yours! You'll have to walk a piece to get to his stable. It's all the way down by Wiley's Swamp.

ICHABOD
I'll find it. Afternoon, Good Mynheer Van Houten, Mevrouw, Juffrouw.

(Crane's traveling music.)

Scene 4.

"He Designed It!"

(ICHABOD AND YOST VAN HOUTEN enter from opposite sides of the stage. They meet at center.)

YOST
Ah, my friend, Mynheer Crane! And to where do your feet take you in such haste?

ICHABOD
I'm on my way to borrow a horse from the Van Ripper's stable. I'm attending a merry-making to be held at the home of Baltus Van Tassel. Do you know it?

YOST
Know it, my good man? I designed it!

ICHABOD
Did you?

YOST
Indeed. I still have the drawings for that particular farm house, if you'd like to see them.

ICHABOD
Some other time, perhaps. Right now, I must procure my horse for the quilting frolic.

YOST

I'm on my way to the very same gathering. Never missed a year. I'll give you a hand up onto the horse. You will need a boost in mounting the beast. Besides, it will give us an opportunity to talk.

(Van Houten takes Ichabod by the arm and begins leading him offstage.)

ICHABOD
Why whatever would we talk about?

YOST
Have you any interest in *architecture*, Mynheer Crane?

ICHABOD
Not especially.

YOST

You see, the Van Tassel home is one of my spacious farmhouses, with high-ridged, but lowly-sloping roofs, built in the style handed-down from the first Dutch settlers. The low projecting eaves form a piazza along the front, which I feel is most…

(They exit as Van Houten continues to enlighten Ichabod Crane on the topic of architecture, more than any reasonable person would care to know. Knickerbocker enters.)

KNICKERBOCKER

Yost Van Houten hoisted Ichabod up onto the horse. Then Ichabod and Gunpowder shambled out of the stable at Wiley's Swamp like such an apparition as is seldom to be met with in broad daylight. Now, Brom Bones' horse was the very antithesis of Ichabod's kerplopping glue factory. And Brom Bones was proud of his stallion. He was consequently the hero of the scene, having come to the gathering on his favorite steed, "Dare-Devil", a creature like Bones himself, full of mettle and mischief, and which no one but himself could manage. He was, in fact, noted for preferring vicious animals, given to all kinds of tricks, which kept the rider in constant risk of his neck, for he held a tractable well-broken horse as unworthy of a lad of spirit. Upon their arrival, the autumnal festivities were in full swing!

Scene 5.

"An Autumn Feast"

(CHEERFUL, CELEBRATORY MUSIC FROM THE period. Baltus Van Tassel enters the new scene. Lights rise on the 'Castle Van Tassel'. Folks bring in baskets of goodies, garlands of autumn leaves to hang, casks of spirits, and delectable Dutch dishes of all kinds. Festive torchlights with a smorgasbord table downstage is center. The guests have arrived in costume and are all in period masque. At a certain moment in music and a physical cue by Van Tassel, everyone surrounds the table with goblets in hand and turn to face Baltus.)

<u>BALTUS</u>

Welcome! Welcome! One and all! You are all welcome to the "Castle Van Tassel" for our annual night of revelry and feasting in this sumptuous season! *(The party guests explode in cheers and whistles.)* Let us not, however, stand on ceremony to the exclusion of nourishment, for our appetites, some more than others, must be satiated in the tradition of an authentic Van Tassel spread. And as I stand here this evening, I am aware that all eyes are open to every symptom of culinary abundance, ranged with delight over the treasures of jolly autumn. So, without further ado, I present my lovely wife to do the honors. Mrs. Van Tassel, what burgeoning cornucopia have you in store for our taste buds this evening?

<u>MRS. VAN TASSEL</u>
(Teasing them all)

Well, Dear, this year I'm afraid to say I haven't prepared much. *(A few jeers and whines of disappointment)* Only enough for the King and Queen of Holland! *(Cheers)*

BALTUS

I'll make my hospitable attentions brief but sincere, confined to a shake of the hand, a slap on the shoulder, a gentle kiss here and there, in order that you can indulge with reckless abandon as I extend a hearty invitation to fall to and help yourselves!

(They cheer. Slow, dreamlike music in. Throughout the rest of Mrs. Van Tassel's speech, she crosses downstage tot 'narrate' the menu for the audience as the party guests dig in behind her. The crowd should mime eating in slow-motion in order to facilitate conveying the passage of time.)

MRS. VAN TASSEL

Now, just feast your eyes upon these porkers, and a carved-out, sleek side of bacon, and juicy relishing ham, behold every turkey daintily trussed up, with gizzards under wings, and peradventure a necklace of savory sausages; And even bright chanticleer himself lay sprawling on his back, in a side-dish with uplifted claws, as if craving that quarter which his chivalrous spirit disdained to ask while living.

(The crowd reacts favorably.)

MRS. VAN TASSEL

Rich wheels of wheat, rolls of rye, baguettes of buckwheat, and crunchy, colorful Indian corn with its golden ears peeping from leafy coverts holding out the promise of cakes and hasty pudding; and the yellow pumpkins lying beneath them, turning up their fair round bellies to the sun, and giving ample prospects of the most luxurious of pies. My orchards are simply burthened with ruddy
fruit!

BALTUS

On all sides, behold a vast store of apples.

JUDITH
Some hanging in oppressive opulence.

NICHOLAUS
Some gathered into baskets and barrels.

YOST
Others heaped up into rich piles.

PARSON
Soon to be pressed into spiced, hot cider.

HILDA
Breathe in the odor of the beehive!

DERRICK
Anticipate the sweet flavor of dainty slapjacks.

JONATHAN
Well buttered and garnished with honey or treacle.

MRS. VAN TASSEL
By the delicate little dimpled hand of our very own daughter, Katrina.

(Another round of oohs and ahhs from the revelers.)

ICHABOD
But now our minds are being fed with many 'tart thoughts' and 'sugared suppositions'.

MRS. VAN TASSEL
And for the sweet tooth, just you dwell upon the ample charms of a genuine Dutch country tea table… Such heaped-up platters of cakes of various and

almost indescribable kinds, imported from the Netherlands, known only to experienced Dutch housewives! There is the doughty doughnut, the crisp and crumbling cruller,…

MORT
…sweet cakes and shortcakes,

JONATHAN
…ginger cakes and honey cakes,

MRS. VAN RIPPER
…and the whole family of cakes,

MRS. VAN RIPPER
…and then there are apple pies,

HILDA
…peach pies,

BROM BONES
…and pumpkin pies,

DERRICK
…strudels and cinnamon wheels,

YOST
…cheeses and chocolates,

BALTUS
…besides slices of ham and smoked beef;

MRS. VEDDER
And moreover delectable dishes of preserved plums,

<u>DOFFUE</u>
…cranberries, pears and quinces,

<u>PETER</u>
…not to mention broiled shad and roasted chickens!

<u>HANS</u>
…together with bowls of milk and cream,

<u>ICHABOD</u>
…all mingled higgledly-piggledy!

Pretty much as I have enumerated them, with the motherly teapot sending up its vapor from the midst – Heaven Bless the Mark!

HEAVEN BLESS THE MARK!

And now shall we continue the night's revels as we are want? The sound of music from the common room summons us to dance! *(cheers from all around)* Let us not see a limb nor fiber that is not in motion! No idle feet here. Dancers! Dancers!

(The dance begins. It is a 'jig' or 'reel' indicative of the time and place. It should be beautifully choreographed and made to look deliberately rehearsed and well-executed. The following should be paired like so; Baltus and Mrs. Van Tassel, Brom Bones and Katrina, Hans and Mrs. Van Ripper, Nicholaus and Mrs. Vedder, Doffue and Anouk, Derrick and Hilda, Ichabod and Judith, Jonathan and Kristina. Mort, the Parson, Peter, Yost, etcetera may all be paired up appropriately with various and sundry female frolickers. Ichabod, at one point gets linked up with Katrina, Brom has to link up to someone else, which incenses him. Ichabod ends up dancing solo. It is a wild and crazy dance, very funny. Dance comes to an end with music. All laugh and applaud accordingly.)

<u>BALTUS</u>

Excellent! Excellent! You would have thought Saint Vitus himself, that blessed patron of the dance, was figuring before us in person. At this time, those who desire it may retire to the piazza where we shall smoke our pipes, drink mulled wine, dole out wild and wonderful legends and spin yarns of ghosts and apparitions. Our chief tale tonight will be that favorite specter of Sleepy Hollow, THE HEADLESS HORSEMAN, who has been heard several times of late, patrolling the country and tethering his horse nightly among the graves in the churchyard! To the piazza!

Scene 6.

"War Stories"

(THE MEN ARE ON THE Van Tassel piazza, while the women are gathered in the foreground in a clearing in front of the Van Tassel home. While the men tell stories of war, the women interject what really happened. This dialogue should be done in alternating fashion with the men oblivious to the wives' words and the wives oblivious to the men's. Both groups are telling stories in different areas, yet simultaneously. After the one group tells their side of a tale, they freeze. The other group will then have full focus from the audience while they speak and react.)

MRS. VAN TASSEL
I can just hear them now. Filling Master Crane's head with pure fiction!

(Ladies agree.)

BALTUS
…you see, Mynheer Crane, this neighborhood, at the time of which I am speaking, was one of those highly favored places which abound with chronicle and great men…

JUDITH
They always make themselves the heroes of every exploit!

(Ladies agree.)

PARSON
…the British and American line had run near it during the war; it had therefore been the scene of marauding, and infested with refugees, cowboys, and all kinds of border chivalry…

MRS. VAN TASSEL
…at the which, our husbands were the first to lock up our doors, and bolt the windows!

(Ladies giggle.)

DOFFUE
…and I had nearly, single-handedly, taken the British frigate with an old iron nine-pounder from a mud breastwork!

(The men ooh and ahh at the story, while the women see it in a different way.)

HILDA
…almost, that is, until my Uncle's gun burst at the sixth discharge!

(Ladies laugh a little more.)

DOFFUE
I was very brave.

HILDA
…He was so frightened, in fact, that upon hearing the British were coming, he pulled the trigger prematurely and alerted the enemy to his regiment's location!

(The ladies fall into great laughter.)

NICHOLAUS
…so I, in the battle of White Plains, being an excellent master of defense, parried a musket ball with a small sword, insomuch that I absolutely felt it whiz 'round the blade and glance off at the hilt!

(The men are really excited by this story.)

MRS. VEDDER

Master of the blade? Yes, he could use a paring knife very well. He was the regiment's cook and could chop carrots, onions, and peppers like no one else!

(Greater laughter now from the ladies.)

HANS

…and I was accounted quite a swordsman in my time during the revolution. In proof of which, I am ready at any time to show my sword with the hilt, a little bent.

MRS. VAN RIPPER

The only cause of his bent sword was getting it caught between his scabbard and the door jam!

(Ladies all burst into loud, hysterical laughter.)

BROM BONES

Enough war stories! I'm sure what Heer Crane would prefer to hear are stories of the Hessian of the Hollow…

ICHABOD

I'm well-acquainted with the spirit soldier so if you'd rather…

BROM BONES

The galloping Hessian is the apparition, no doubt, of an errant jockey who, believing his killer amongst the people of Sleepy Hollow, rides on a mission of vengeance. Perhaps Heer Crane fought in the war. He's certainly old enough to have done so. Is that why you've come to town, Crane? Is it fate that brings you and the Headless Horseman together? Were you the cannon gunner who beheaded the soldier? Is it you, he seeks? The blade of a sabre clutched in his boney grip? I once encountered the phantom. On returning one night from the neighboring village of Sing Sing. I had been overtaken by the midnight trooper. He had offered to race with him for a bowl of punch, and should have won it, too. But Daredevil beat the goblin horse all Hollow. And just as we came to the old bridge, the specter turned into a skeleton, and bolted away over the treetops with a clap of thunder and a flash of FIRE!

(Crane withdraws his pocketwatch.)

ICHABOD

Well, just look at the time. I really should be going. I'll just find Vrouw Katrina and perhaps she'll want to take a nice moonlit stroll.

BROM BONES

Be careful, Schoolmaster. The Hollow isn't safe after midnight. And it's already one-thirty of the clock.

ICHABOD

Your concern for my health, Brom Bones, gives one pause.

(A little music and all guests exit. Ichabod sees Katrina at a punch bowl and joins her. Brom Bones soon follows and joins the two. During Knickerbocker's speech, Katrina is seen speaking to Crane. She returns to Ichabod, the book he once gave her. She then takes Brom Bones' arm and exits with the younger, handsomer man.)

KNICKERBOCKER

The revel now gradually broke up. Ichabod only lingered behind, according to the custom of country lovers, to have a tete-a-tete with the heiress, fully convinced that he was now on the high road to success. What passed at this interview, I will not pretend to say. For in fact I do not know. Something, however, I fear me, must have gone wrong for he certainly sallied forth with an heir quite desolate and chopfallen. Ichabod stole forth with the heir of one who had been sacking a hen roost rather than a fair lady's heart.

Scene 7.

"The Very Witching Time of Night"

(Ichabod enters, whistling nervously. He stops at Center.)

ICHABOD

It is the very witching time of night that I, Ichabod Crane, heavy-hearted and crestfallen, pursue my travel homeward. All those stories of ghosts and goblins come crowding now upon my recollection. The night grows darker and darker. The stars seem to sink deeper in the sky and driving clouds hide them from my sight. I have never felt more lonely, nor dismal.

(The three apparitions; Major Andre, Starkenfaust, and the Snow Maiden, materialize in clouds of smoke and ghoulish green under-lighting, upstage of Crane. They begin moaning direfully. Crane hears but does not see them yet. In fear, he shouts…)

Angels and ministers of grace, defend us! Come Gunpowder!

KNICKERBOCKER

But Gunpowder took off into the night,… *(Sound of galloping horse's hooves, then fading as it goes off into the distance.)* leaving the schoolmaster without a horse upon which to make it home. The pedagogue ventured deeper into the dark wood in search of his steed.

ICHABOD
Gunpowder?

KNICKERBOCKER

In the center of the clearing, stood an enormous tree, which towered like a giant above all the other trees of the neighborhood and formed a kind of landmark.

It was universally known by the nane of "Major Andre's Tree". Unbeknownst to Crane, he was approaching the very place where many of the scenes of the ghost stories shad been laid.

(Knickerbocker exits.)

ICHABOD
Gunpowder?! Come here, Boy!

(He attempts to whistle the horse back.)

Heer Van Ripper will be awfully perturbed if I return with your reigns and no horse underneath… GUNPOWDER?!

(He sees something. Light intensifies on the tree.)

Where am I now? Could this be the tree of Major Andre?

Scene 8.

"Three Apparitions"

(*CRANE BACKS AWAY FROM IT. Music builds in anticipation of the impending horror. Lights gradually intensify, illuminating the figure. It is now very clearly obvious that it is the still and lifeless form of Major Andre hanging from a noose.*)

My senses further betray me. This is no apparition! The tree has merely been scathed by lightning and the white wood laid bare.

(*In an instant the corpse springs to life. Andre jerks his head in the direction of the pedagogue, opens his possessed, colorless eyes, darting them directly at Crane. Andre lets loose with a terrifying scream. Crane screams and hides his eyes from the horrifying visage. The Snow Maiden and Starkenfaust laugh maniacally.*)

<u>MAJOR ANDRE</u>

FOOL! Dare you doubt my existence and turn your eyes from the truth of death?! Mark this tree well, Pedagogue! For my tragical story is carved into its very trunk with tales of strange sights and doleful lamentations. Feast your eyes upon my horrible visage! Regard my corrupt corpse, decaying in the wood, worm-infested, and strung up in this mighty arbor where I have been left forever to rot in history! Hear my moans, Ichabod Crane,… (*Demonstrates a chilling moan*) as they blast forth, sweeping sharply through bristles and dry branches. Damned be your arrogance for entering this cursed ground! Let fear become your master, for…

> as your bones clatter
> and your teeth chatter,
> your knees will rattle
> against your saddle!

(The three apparitions howl in pain to further frighten Crane. Andre then expels a ghastly death rattle, closes his eyes and returns to his lifeless form. Underlighting on the Snow Maiden rises to an eerie green.

ICHABOD

In the dank mists of the forest's fog, I behold a thing, white, mysterious, floating upon the air? No, it is simply some shrub covered with snow and like a sheeted spectre, tricks the reason of my eyes. Avaunt and quit my sight, foul foliage!

SNOW MAIDEN

(Suddenly screams in agony. She then speaks to Crane as if from a deep, dark crypt.)

Ichabod Crane, 'tis I, the Snow Maiden of Raven Rock. Hear my heart-broken voice. Look upon my skeletal visage, frozen with a final countenance of terror, tears of ice splintered long ago in the bitter wind that stole my life. Caress my cracked and lesioned skin. Run your fingers through my matted hair, encrusted with frosty nests of sleeping grubs. Embrace my stiffened sinew and brittle bones, kiss my leathery lips, and taste the sweet death of my breath, tainted with the stench of rotted flesh. Touch my arms, and legs. Feel my longing for life. Bloodless now and corrupt, my corpse has withered with the years. I, a victim of winter's cruelty. Surely *you* see the beauty in my hideousness. Come, Ichabod, make love to me, take my hand and come with us. Share with us our eternal home in Hell. Die with me, lie with me in my cold, cold, crypt of ice!

> The horseman dealt his head a blow –
> His bones fell fast, a bloody heap.
> Maiden's hands emerged from snow,
> and pulled her lover down six feet deep!

ICHABOD

No!!! It cannot be! You are not real! It is no frost-bitten hag I see! No white witch I hear! This descent into madness is the issue of my own thoughts!

(Underlighting on Starkenfaust rises to an eerie green. He speaks.)

STARKENFAUST

Mark me, Crane… Lend a careful ear to my words. For I, Hermann Von Starkenfaust, am that very horseman without a skull. Hessian of Germany, commissioned by the British to fight in the great war. You see me now as I was in life. Regard my head firmly affixed upon strong shoulders and head my words… Your only chance of survival in these woods from my demonic incarnation is the bridge. To pass the bridge is the severest trial. For when I ride head-less, my horse is fast and my aim, expert. But once you cross, you have 'scaped with your life. My horse cannot follow that which reaches the other side. Pray I don't dismount and pursue you on foot! For many have crossed the haunted stream never to return. Fearful are the feelings of every schoolboy who passes it alone after dark. Beware my headless form, Ichabod Crane. Lest it creep up from behind and take you down, down to dusty death!

He that supper for is dight'
He'll lie full cold, I swear this night!
Off to bedchamber I, him, lead.
This night, gray-steel shall make his bed!

(Starkenfaust wails as a ghost. He senses the awakening of the undead.)

Scene 9.

"The Stalking Dead"

(FROM OUT OF TRAP DOORS, secret hovels, and shallow graves, boney hands begin to tear away from their confinements as if awakening from a sleep of several hundred years. Corpses, the 'stalking dead' begin to claw their way out.)

THREE APPARITIONS

Behold you now, the souls departed from this world. Churchyards yawn and clandestine graves gape wide to unleash these Hell-bound hearts of the undead. How they stir from charnel beds and tear themselves loose from their eternal inferno! They awake disturbed, as you tread upon this cursed ground beneath which they once slept!

ICHABOD

Yet, is there more?! The trees of the grove now seem to surround me. Their limbs, gnarled and twisted and appear to take on the personification of the those inhabitants of Sleepy Hollow… They are not trees! They are the stalking dead! The damned burst forth from yawning grave yards and risen to cast a warning. Speak! You terrors of the night! SPEAK!

(During the monologue above, the stalking dead continue to drag and hobble their half-working bodies ever so slowly, over to Ichabod Crane. They moan and groan as if struggling with the half-living, half-dead state of their physiology. Crane is, all this time rooted to the spot in paralyzing fear. Many of the corpses appear to be falling apart, dropping limbs and dried-up, vital organs along the way. Creepy music swells underneath while the three apparition impart the following warning in verse.)

THREE APPARITIONS / STALKING DEAD

*("Horseman of the Hollow" by Christofer Cook. Copyright, 2002.
All rights reserved.)*

Beware the Headless Horseman,
On a nightly quest he rides.
To avenge his gruesome murder,
In the darkest wood he hides.

He's coming for you at a quarter to two,
Ride fast, you may survive.
But if you tarry, for the weight you carry,
You'll no more be seen alive!

Clop, clop, clop,
His horse will never stop!
Chop, chop, chop,
His blade is sure to lop…

The scalp of your head,
The nape of your neck,
The mass above your chest.

You'll bleed bright red,
He'll leave you for dead,
Your corpse, there laid to rest.

Closer and closer,
You can hear the goblin's cape
Closer and closer,
You're his, there's no escape!

He's on you now,
He *HAS* you now!
You pray it's just a dream.

But your mind is sound,
Don't turn around.
All that's left to do is scream!

Scene 10.

"The Headless Horseman"

(THE HEADLESS HORSEMAN ENTERS. WHEN the staking dead and apparitions sense his arrival, they all gradually exit back into their graves and hovels. Crane is now left alone with the horseman. The horseman carries at his side, holding by the hair, a freshly-severed head. Blood streams from the torn strips of sinew emanating from the throat. The Hessian stands majestically. He slowly begins closing proximity. Music rises…)

ICHABOD

If I can but reach that bridge, I am safe! I shall run through to the opposite end. For the goblin will surely hurl his severed head at me!

(Crane attempts to run away, he is circled by the Headless Horseman who is also at this point on foot. The Horseman tosses the severed head offstage and Crane stupidly charges the horseman like a bull. The horseman holds the pumpkin at waist-level, the stem facing the horseman's navel. When the top of the pedagogue's head makes contact with the bottom of the pumpkin, it punches through and Crane pulls off from the horseman. Crane is now wearing the entire pumpkin like a mask. He runs around blindly, attempting to pull the gourd off, but to no avail. The horseman gets Crane on the ground and drags him by the feet off stage. Music mixes into the next scene.)

Epilogue

(THE CHAOS FROM THE ENCOUNTER with the Headless Horseman, the night before, dies out. Morning music and lighting gently ease in. Enter the Van Tassels and Van Rippers. All carry lit lanterns as if having spent the previous dark hours of the morning searching about.)

BALTUS
Goedemorgen, Mynheer, Van Ripper.

HANS
Goedemorgen, Mynheer Van Tassel.

BALTUS
Any Word?

HANS
None.

MRS. VAN RIPPER
Heer Crane did not make appearance at breakfast.

HANS
An inquiry has been set on foot and the constable has called for a diligent inquest. His volunteers are arriving just now.

(Enter Van Houten, Vanderdonk, and Vedders.)

YOST
The horse was found but no saddle.

PETER
The bridle and reins on the leaves at the horse's hooves.

(Enter Sleepy Hollow Boys and others.)

BROM BONES
We checked the schoolhouse but no Mynheer Crane.

MRS. VEDDER
We searched the brook…

NICHOLAUS
…the body of the schoolmaster was not to be discovered.

PARSON
He's not in the church.

HILDA
But on one part of the road leading to the graveyard,…

DOFFUE
…we found his saddle trampled in the dirt,…

HILDA
…Heer Crane's hat, and close beside it, a shattered pumpkin.

KATRINA
He's gone.

BALTUS
Hans Van Ripper, you're the executor of Crane's estate.
What has he left behind?

MRS. VAN RIPPER
We've examined the bundle which contained all his worldly effects.

HANS
And we found,…*(He pulls each item out of Ichabod's tied-up cloth, then Mrs. Van Ripper takes each item and places it into an old brown cloth sack.)* Two shirts and a half, two neck stocks, a couple of worsted stockings, an old pair of corduroy pantaloons, a rusty razor, a much dog-eared book of psalm tunes, and a broken pitch pipe. These items I'll divvy among those in need.

MRS. VAN RIPPER
As to the books and furniture of the schoolhouse,
they belong to the community.

HANS
However, the books on music, fortune-telling, dreams, this *Cotton Mather's History of Witchcraft* – I shall consign all these books to the flames from whence they came. From this time forward I am determined to send my children no more to school. I never knew way good come of this same reading and writing anyway.

KRISTINA
What's happened to the man?

MRS. VAN TASSEL
It's obvious he flew from the place from a broken heart.

BROM BONES
He was presumptuous. And that led to his demise.

MRS. VEDDER
He was no doubt spirited away by supernatural means.

JUDITH

Abducted by the galloping Hessian and cast into the underworld.

PARSON

Poor damned soul. We must continue our search
that he may be interred in consecrated ground.

(Gentle music eases in and underscores the following.)

KNICKERBOCKER

As he was a bachelor and in nobody's debt, no one troubled his head about the schoolmaster anymore. Brom Bones, shortly after his rival's disappearance, conducted the blooming Katrina in triumph to the alter. He was observed to look exceedingly knowing whenever the story of Ichabod was related, which led some to suspect that he knew more about the matter than he chose to tell. Still, it remains a mystery. For that fateful night, the Headless Horseman was believed to have met up with Ichabod Crane at the very same time Abraham Van Brunt was courting the young Katrina. The schoolhouse, being deserted, soon fell to decay and was reported to be haunted by the unfortunate pedagogue. The inhabitants of Tarry Town, loitering homeward of a still autumn evening, often fancy his voice at a distance, chanting a melancholy psalm tune among the tranquil solitudes of Sleepy Hollow.

(Fog creeps in with mysterious music. Ensemble moves in slow motion with lit lanterns, as ambient light all around them dims. Their movement should convey villagers in search of a missing person. At an appropriate moment, the cast freezes into dramatic tableau. Fog, music, continues as ambient lighting fades completely to black, leaving the lanterns' points of light all aglow.)

END OF PLAY

www.ingramcontent.com/pod-product-compliance
Lightning Source LLC
LaVergne TN
LVHW011844060526
838200LV00054B/4152